Yoke

Poems by Caiti Quatmann

a MyrtleHaus
publication

For Mike and Wade

"I assumed this yoke would encase me as well as any another hobble, only this one bound the mind."

—Jazz Feylynn, *Prismatic Prose: A Genre Bending Anthology*

TABLE OF CONTENTS

—✦—

PHONE CALLS

After Matt Rasmussen

Your son is dead
but you don't know yet.

Your husband dials
his phone again,

his fingers creak—
aged wood, dried out

from the mundane
wear of daily life.

You remember
the days they blushed

with youth,
entwined around your hand.

Everything has grown
old and rickety.

Except for his voice,
quivering with anticipation

like the clumsy teen
from when you first met.

MEMORIAL

he

died

and

we   stand

numb

surviving   in

sin

[1] Text from https://www.findagrave.com/memorial/18530210/wade-samuel-steffey

7

AFTER TRAGEDY

A campus is nothing
but the lives that move

within it. Wade trudged
through winter's embrace;

snowflakes fell
through the night

gathering silently
on the ground, concealing

his footsteps. The space
between the dorm

and darkness, one foot
in the buzz of college

life, one in the silence.
He couldn't hear the calls—

our shouting, the searching—
frozen in the bitter air.

I wanted to step
into the silence,

trace the invisible path
he wandered through,

halt the snow
so he could stand again,

but my heart held
as if anchored in ice.

The snow on the ground
reflected the moon

and then became it, rose upward
and outward, filling every footprint,

sealing the quiet,
leaving only night.

SEARCH PARTY

The authorities collected
the jacket you'd left

in our dorm room,
the keys it harbored.

They gathered us at the station,
instructed us on the art of the grid:

relay only what our eyes captured,
resist the allure of touching.

Our journey began by the stadium,
progressing down toward campus.

We found a shoe by the now infamous door;
We told them it looked like yours.

Perhaps it was the magic you used to gain entry
because, supposedly, it was impenetrable;

they'd sworn no one could access
the building from there. Yet,

months later, there you were.
Imprisoned behind a sealed door,

a single shoe on your foot;
rotting, charred, and lifeless.

BUBBLES

We met in my dorm—a routine pre-game,
youthful spirits eager to escape

the confining walls and nascent jolts
of unfolding adulthood.

In the kitchen, a pot bubbled, vapors
mingling with our anticipation.

We shared plates of ramen, swigs of liquor,
the table a mismatched patchwork,

used dishes and scuffed flatware.
We roamed familiar paths together,

the evening chill kissing our faces,
breath visible in the frigid air.

We ventured, compelled by the distant throb,
music and revelry—that siren call—

wading into a sea of bubbles.
Inside the frat was a tempest,

colors and sound, bodies entangled.
The basement was slick from sweat and foam.

We danced, bubbles popping against our skin,
the music's pulse propelling us forward.

As the night progressed and the foam thinned,
We found ourselves outside, shivering

in the late evening air. Someone asked
Where is Wade? Has anybody seen him?

And we shook our heads.
You'd probably left

or were still inside dancing.
And the following morning,

after the bubble of night had burst,
and we had cleaned ourselves, we still

were left with a tacky film, and unresolved
questions, and the budding chasm of your

absence. Our calls went straight to voicemail,
filling up the box; your coat and keys

slouched on my roommate's chair,
and we finally began to worry.

FALLING

The timid dawn spills its gray light
over the quiet corners of the world.

It settles on the branches, the leaves,
the grass; fills the silence with a solemn line,

a frail blue story
of the day barely begun.

What is the warmth of the sun,
that golden glow compared to this—

this tumbling of a tiny life
from the safety of its nest.

A flutter, too soon, too frail—
a dance in mid-air, falling

down through the layers of dawn.
The bird touches the earth.

Then the breeze whispering soft
through the bough, then pausing,

then stirring again, lifting
lightly—the stillness;

then the morning lays its
dewy tears upon the ground.

THINGS WE DID AFTER YOUR DEATH

We couldn't bear to mention your name,
the one that inked each day's headlines...*Promising*

Young Student Goes Missing; 10 Days
Gone; A Month and No Answers...

We had read them all, of course. The exposé
wondering if it was murder—a serial killer

targeting drunken young men on college campuses,
wading the length of the Midwest from La Crosse,

down the Mississippi, then crossing to the Wabash.
Relentless, muddy flows, carrying young dead men

past sleepy towns, or hiding stories beneath the currents. Too
many bodies to be chalked up to falling in. I can't remember

if they trudged the Wabash looking for you. At the time
we all thought it—he's probably dead. But we never said it

aloud, like saying the words, giving breath to the notion would be
what finally killed you. In the first moment we didn't yet know,

so we kept drinking Natty Light frothing in red polystyrene;
we floated to class, across the campus that felt forever changed

yet looked the same: the leaves clung stubbornly to the trees,
orange and red against a steel-gray sky, refusing to let go.

We did laundry not knowing you were entombed
across the hall. The rhythmic whir and soapy aroma,

an island of normalcy in a sea of uncertainty.
We folded clothes, mechanically occupying our hands

while our minds wandered the corridors;
for all we knew, you would walk back

into our dorm room, and ask Andrea if
she wanted to do chemistry homework,

just like I heard you do most Thursday afternoons for
the last five months. And by then, you would have been

studying for midterms, anyways,
holed up in the library for days.

THE WILD

In the quiet after rain, time whispers.
It's in the way the mist clings to the mountains—

a memory too heavy to lift.
The trees, old souls keeping vigil;

stoic witnesses, their roots
tangled in centuries.

There is a stillness here,
a pause between one breath

and the next—where even the river seems
to hold its tongue, bearing witness

to the slow dance of the stars.
Beneath the surface, under layers

of earth and history, secrets sleep
in their own rhythm, unhurried

by the tick of human clocks. They speak
in the language of leaves unfurling,

of silent seeds bursting into stubborn life.
Sometimes, in the half-light of dawn,

the world feels like a question left
unanswered. The vastness of the sky,

a blank page, where clouds drift, unscripted,
and the horizon blurs the line between knowing

and wondering. Here, in the endless cycle
of bloom and wither, time doesn't march;

it breathes. It's in the hawk's circling shadow,
the rustle of grass as unseen creatures pass,

and the steady gaze of the mountain,
witnessing years as moments.

And in this expanse, I am a wanderer,
footsteps echoing in the vast cathedral

of the wild, each step overshadowed
by the mysteries that outlast us;

the ones we carry
in our bones

but never quite grasp.

REMEMBERING

Lately I find myself remembering,
pouring over article after article,

questioning the role I unwittingly
played in the narrative.

Your disappearance. Your death,
splashed across each headline.

I place myself in them, there
in 2007, that fateful January—

my name whispered in corridors,
blamed for an invitation, a party's list—

the night that spiraled beyond foresight.
And the door, infamous and pivotal,

its handle frosted and seasoned,
a threshold to paths unforeseen.

I venture into the labyrinth of collective
memory, fumbling and wading through

the stories, probing for absolution among
misplaced blame. Murmurs of accusation,

the vaporous judgments that betray my steps,
drawing me into the closet of public scrutiny.

Our rapport, tenuous yet indelible, brief and
decisive, like the swift, unforgiving strike of fate

that shocked the foundation of my college life,
wedged us in a closet of communal grief,

confined and lost among unasked questions.
Time's river flows—days into months, into years

and still, the echoes of that night linger.
The door to closure stands untouched, unopened,

your absence a specter, a septic fragrance of
unresolved mysteries drifting

through the halls of our shared history.
It pleads with the living,

with me, to unravel the tangles,
to find solace in the midst of lingering chaos,

a whisper in the dark, seeking light.

HIDE AND SEEK

You, wandering in the gathering night,
seeking admittance; while we dance,

our bodies sweat too much for a winter's night.
Too loud to hear our phones, to see your texts.

No way to grab your things from our room.
You try anyway, finding an open door

among the rear—dark, unadorned, yet inviting enough.
You venture into the indomitable chamber,

all while we grope each other, encased in bubbles—
in total darkness, fumbling for any pathway. You hear

the persistent murmur of transformers
in their night-song, as we drown

our thoughts in cheap beer and loud music,
tripping over limbs and soap. You falter,

unseen wires betray your steps and
draw you into the closet's depths.

Your first and only contact
with the transformer—a final kiss

shocking you dead. Wedged against a brick wall,
you fall lifeless, trapped in the utility closet.

You're missing, but we don't know that yet.
We eventually head back, stumbling the same path,

tripping into bed, sleeping off the night.
And then for weeks, that door stands untouched,

unopened. Until your putrid miasma drifts
down the hallway, reminding the living: I'm still here.

THE CUSTODIAN'S DISCOVERY

During a routine check
(my nightly sweep)

the room's popping
pulls at my steps.

The charged air rhythmically
pulsing, accented by a clawing scent,

a morbid fusion. There,
where darkness meets faint light,

you lay still.
My hands tremble,

unprepared. I move closer;
a pungent onslaught:

decay and burnt flesh.
My eyes blur, rebelling.

A swell of nausea,
the taste of bile,

bitter and acrid. Your shape
turns grotesque. Mottled

greens, blues, and yellows—shades
previously unknown to me

paint the stretched canvas of
your peeling, charred skin.

LICHTENBERG FIGURES

After particles collide,
an electric field forms

among the heavens;
conductive pathways

furiously descending,
branching down from

the charged sky, unveiling
a spark that propels it.

A bolt, arcing;
it traces a jagged path,

etching a fierce line
through the breathless air

until it severs one branch;
the tree's spine cracks open.

Before the leaves tremble,
the lightning unfurls,

a blazing electric lance
then again it's sky-bound,

recoiling from its intrusion
through the bark.

Its scarred trail
resting in the trunk

of a sturdy oak to linger
like veins. I touch it;

all the leaves shiver
and pulse with heat.

NECROMANCY

The winds pick up,
reanimating the dead

leaves cuddling together
atop the church's steeple.

They glide from their slumber,
painting the too-blue sky

with crumpled taupes and
burnt siennas, wallpapering

the air, as arms reach toward
the heavens—impish limbs,

auspicious hands—turning up
to embrace the last remnants of fall,

petitioning for a small
communion with nature.

THE DEAD LAY UPON THE LIVING

The dead lay upon the living,
their full weight sprawled atop our bodies;

they are missionaries journeying across realms
to bestow upon us this grief;

cruelly murmuring in our ears
to enlighten us through death.

Their calls resonate within our flesh,
tracing the perimeters of our hearts,

reverberating in chambers of loss and remembrance;
we, the ones shouldering the load of their absence,

the mass of empty expanses filled with
the unspoken, the incomplete, the unknowable;

we interlace their absence into our beings,
knot by knot, strand by strand, until

the load is endurable. And, the world lives on:
the wind continues rustling leaves,

and the sun and moon persist
in their infernal choreography.

OBITUARY

unexpected loss ... his ... Grim ... tending ... is ... A ... Cruelty ... visit ... Home

AFTER SUICIDE

What did you become,
if wood becomes charcoal,

after the flames died?
I take the charcoal

of your ashes.
I draw you

over and over.
Infinite realities

crafted from
your bones.

Now you can
live forever.

DANDELIONS

In the meadow behind our house,
where wild things converge,

we would play. My brother
and I, in sunlight bathed,

golden crowns upon the grass,
their fleeting reign beaconing.

The dandelions, humble earth stars,
white-tufted heads, full of seeds,

with each soft exhale, a scattering—
our eyes closed, a wish to make—

tiny voyagers released. The seeds
took to the air, small paragliders,

each carrying the childhood promise
of magic. Sailing the winds,

they journeyed to unknowns,
open and unbroken. Now,

returning alone, I hold a dandelion,
its head bowed with age.

The field lies still.
I murmur a wish,

and set the seeds adrift
into the winds of memory,

carried away, into
the harsh daylight.

A PHONE CALL

When you first started being dead,
I was helping Mom take down wallpaper

(she was preparing to sell the house), and
the phone rang. It was just after Thanksgiving,

which you were supposed to attend,
but never showed. It wasn't unlike you

to ghost us, so we hadn't
worried too much. Between

the snow and your unreliability, maybe
you'd figured it was safer to not come.

I had answered the phone
as Mom stripped the walls;

the police officer on the line asked
if we knew you; when had we seen you.

I kept watching Mom work at the top of the ladder
(the kitchen ceilings being so high),

and I wished you were there to help.
You had always been so tall.

I passed her the phone, and stared at
the naked wall. Its skin peeled away.

BODY FOUND IN NEW MEXICO

They say you are a burned body.
They say they found you in a canal,

charred, and hidden from
the world. Instead, I imagine

you on a gondola.
Someone else,

they called it a culvert.
And I imagine you as a troll.

The police told us
they found you

on the side of the road;
I imagine you hitchhiking.

What none of them will say outright:
you are dead; you killed yourself.

So, I imagine you alive. And I look for you:
near streams and rivers; under bridges;

at every street corner,
or on each highway.

Because searching
is still easier than

asking questions
you can never answer.

SCORCHED EARTH

After heat stirs
a flame awakens

amidst the wilds;
winding pathways

fiercely ascending,
climbing up from

the parched earth.
The fire, spreading;

it traces a relentless path
carving a merciless line

through the gasping land
until it engulfs one tree;

The timber's bark chars.
Before the leaves wither

the wildfire unfurls
a raging inferno's tongue.

Then again it's earth-bound,
spreading from its birth

through the brush.
A scorched trail razing

the forest, making way
for new growth.

IN THE LIBRARY

I went alone to the library in search of anything
to help me to understand your final act.

I sat reading about arson and immolation.
It was newly autumn. The day grew darker early

and the library was filled with umbrellas,
sweaters and trench coats, glasses, and old books.

You were gone to a place of no return
so I searched for answers by reading historical accounts

and slowly I absorbed the narratives:
the monks in Vietnam—still, and then aflame;

Jan Palach, protesting with his life.
Ordinary people compelled through extraordinary pain

sacrificing themselves to hopefully ignite a spark in others.
Their reasons were complex. I read them all

without pause—too focused to stop.
Then I considered the date and time:

the relentless march of days and hours.
Suddenly, from within, came a sigh of anguish,

not very loud or long. It wasn't unexpected;
even then, I already knew the world

was full of suffering. I might have
felt despair, but I didn't.

What shocked me was that it was us:
from my sigh, in my chest.

Without thinking at all, I was you.
I—you—we, we were consumed, our eyes fixed

on the pages of history, full of flames. I said to myself:
on any other day, the pain will still be there.

I was saying it to halt the sensation of being swallowed
by the vast, unfeeling universe. But I felt it:

you are an I, you too are a unique soul,
you are one of them now. So how could I...be you?

I dared not to consider what it meant
to be alive. I cast a furtive glance

(I couldn't look directly) at the surrounding stillness,
the quiet readers and the books, the soft glow of the lamps.

I knew of nothing as strange that had ever happened,
nothing as incomprehensible that ever could;

why should I be my friend, or me, or anyone? What similarities—
pain, loss, the human voice I felt in my chest, or even

the history of self-immolation and all those desperate
final acts—what bound us all together or made us all the same?

How had I come to be, like them,
and bear witness to a sigh of anguish that

could have grown loud and worse and yet it hadn't?
The library was hushed and too still.

It felt as if it was sinking down
beneath a dark wave and another, and another.

Then I was back in it, the world;
it had continued. Outside, in the quiet,

the somber town was dressed in night
and leaves and chill,

and it was still today,
and it was still

the present moment.

SERAPHIC REVERIE

Shadows play on the edges
of clipped wings—a refracted grace,

falling like the last leaves of autumn.
This seraph (once an empyrean creature)

expelled from paradise,
grounded in earthly sorrow.

His eyes, once alight with the fire of stars,
reflect back innocence interrupted

by the sharpness of mortality. This angel,
a blend of shadow and regret, mirroring

the heartache of every soul left behind
(not to the grandiosity of myth but

the quiet tragedies that unfold in
the unseen corners of everyday life).

And the moment the news arrives, the world
retreats into the starkness of black and white.

This cursed dichotomy of memory—how
the laughter and whispers of youth become

both a sanctuary and a torment.
The fallen angels with outstretched hand,

reaching for a heaven we can no longer touch,
yearning to return to days unmarred by grief.

RETREATING

After the storm, the forest exhales;
pine needles glisten like a thousand tiny mirrors

reflecting fragments of a sky, newly washed.
The creek, swollen with rain, carries leaves

that have seen empires rise and fall,
their veins etched with history.

Moss clings to the rocks,
a velvet embrace charting

a history in shades of green and time,
an archive of silence in the undergrowth.

A heron stands—on the water's surface, its reflection
a ghost, touched by the morning's hesitant light.

Shadows play across the bark of a birch, secrets
scripted in fleeting rays, a dialect of darkness and light.

In the meadow, wildflowers awaken;
their petals—open arms, stretching to

a sun that has watched
civilizations turn to dust.

The air vibrates
with the hum of bees.

The mountain, in its stoic grandeur,
wears scars of time like badges,

traces of earth's deep breaths.
And there, in the heart of the wilderness,

where the horizon kisses the sky,
lies the boundary of our understanding,

A frontier that retreats as we approach.

ROASTING

It's been almost two decades
and I still think of you burning.

We make a fire on the patio,
and I see my son through the flames.

His fire hair looks like yours,
as it undulates around his face.

He laughs before poking his stick
in the pit, slowly turning it.

And I wonder what it would be
like to be the marshmallow at

the end. It swells inside as the
skin browns; its sugary flesh spills

out of the casing. It bubbles
and balloons. He holds it

too close, and now it's burning.
"Oops, that's ok though!" he says.

He draws the stick
to his mouth before

blowing out the flames.
The skin is now ash.

I IMAGINE YOU AS A FIRE EATER

In my mind, I rewrite your death:
the match strikes slowly,

reluctant ballet of friction
ushering in a small, quivering flame.

You toy with it reverently,
gingerly. The blaze casts erratic shadows

as you guide it to your lips. Each flicker,
a swallowed memory; each ember,

a sorrow rewritten, a torment healed.
The cinders on your skin begin to cool.

In this version, you conquer the fire—
you draw the flame into your mouth,

your essence glowing amidst the darkness.
The flames inside ricochet against your flesh

yearning for rebirth, seeking comfort.
With a final, triumphant exhale

you release the fire from your lungs;
breathing out the chaos

mending what was broken—
and you live.

WITHERING

The weary sun drapes
its amber over the fading land.

It caresses the petals, the stems,
the leaves; weaves a lament

of a muted crimson saga,
of the season drawing close.

What are the vibrant colors of spring,
those vivid bursts against this—

this wilting of delicate blossoms
beneath the weight of time?

A droop, too soon, too weary—
a descent into the inevitable, withering

beneath the gaze of the evening sky.
The flowers bow to the earth.

Then the wind, murmuring low
through the garden, then stilling,

then breathing once more, carrying
away the remnants;

then the dusk scatters its
frosty sighs upon the ground.

IF WE COULD REWIND

The halo of smoke on your white, charged bones
would dissipate, as muscle and flesh regenerate

among the inferno engulfing your body; blood and
body combining again as one, arisen from the pyre;

the flames would condense into the match head,
which you strike backwards and place in its box;

the putrid smell of gasoline on
your soaked clothes evaporates,

and the petrol flows up into the canister's
long snout held high above your head;

you lower it to your side, walking backward
towards the gas station, returning

the can and its contents, before
heading to the bus stop, where

you retreat to the last seat for the cross-country trip
back to your apartment, and your fire-red hair

that sits in the sink would fly up to your bald head,
roots attaching as the clippers glide forward

across your scalp, returning row after
row of your magnificent auburn mane;

when finally, you would pick up the phone,
reminding us: I'll be there for Thanksgiving dinner.

MISSING YOU IS HARD TO MASTER

Unbeknownst to us, you vanished,
absent. Absent from lectures. Absent

from work. Absent from Thanksgiving.
The windshield wipers absent from your car

though winter reigned in Wisconsin.
Absent your coat. Absent your hair.

We overlooked the signs.
We missed the lies,

the absences you hid.
And I don't know how to miss you

when absence still wears your silhouette.
It's all that composes you now:

the empty chair at the dinner table;
the silence in the cold which

settles more forcefully each winter;
absent from phone calls

and the family group chat
(Mom still sucks at texting btw);

absent from my wedding photos;
absent from your nephew's life;

from holidays at Mom and Dad's
(well, Grandma and Grandpa now)

when we light the same old firepit and
try not to speak about all that's missing.

AUTHOR'S NOTE

This collection is an exploration of two tragic deaths from my teenage years. Two young men who are forever yoked in my memory.

The first was a college friend—a familiar face in our shared circles—whose sudden disappearance and accidental death left our group grappling with questions that had no answers.

The second was the disappearance and death of my brother's best friend, a constant presence in our family since childhood. His life had intertwined with ours. I considered him a brother. His passing, under equally tragic and harrowing circumstances, left a void not just in our family, but in our very sense of reality. The investigation, drawn out and inconclusive, labeled his death a probable suicide.

This book is a journey through the tangled underbrush of loss—an exploration of the impact of these departures on the fabric of my life. It is an attempt to navigate the complex emotions that accompany such profound losses—the disbelief, the search for meaning, and the often impossible acceptance of the inexplicable.

ACKNOWLEDGEMENTS

"The Dead Lay Upon the Living" was written as part of
the First Line Poets Project, created by
Emma-Jane Barlow.
Thank you to Adrian who read this over and over for me,
and for being a constant source of
inspiration and friendship.

As always, immense love and gratitude to my husband, who
is my safe harbor and support in all
things.

ABOUT THE AUTHOR

Caiti Quatmann is a disabled writer and artist in St. Louis, MO. Quatmann's poems and essays have appeared in *LitBreak Magazine*, *The Metaphysical Review*, *Threads Lit Mag*, ASDA's *Tipping Points Magazine*, and others.

Caiti works as a teacher and editor. She is an Editor-in-Chief at the *HNDL Mag* and a teacher at Juniper Root Woodland Microschool.

Outside work, she wanders the woods with her two young children and attempts to convince her husband to adopt a dog.

Follow her work on Instagram and Threads @CaitiTalks

MYRTLEHAUS PUBLISHING

~

MyrtleHaus Publishing stands as a remarkable queer, woman-owned endeavor. Born from the mission to address the lack of representation of women in St. Louis's literary community, MyrtleHaus has grown beyond Missouri's borders, resonating with audiences worldwide. As an independent publishing house, it warmly welcomes submissions of poetry books, anthologies, and novellas, supporting diverse voices and narratives. Complementing this initiative, MyrtleHaus Magazine publishes luxurious, full-length issues biannually. The central mission of MyrtleHaus revolves around creating inclusive and safe publications, championing artists, writers, and small/independent businesses, with a special focus on empowering women, people of color, members of the LGBTQ+ community, and individuals with disabilities.